Dear Parents:

Congratulations! Your child is taking the first steps on an exciting journey. The destination? Independent reading!

STEP INTO READING® will help your child get there. The program offers five steps to reading success. Each step includes fun stories and colorful art or photographs. In addition to original fiction and books with favorite characters, there are Step into Reading Non-Fiction Readers, Phonics Readers and Boxed Sets, Sticker Readers, and Comic Readers—a complete literacy program with something to interest every child.

Learning to Read, Step by Step!

Ready to Read   Preschool–Kindergarten
• big type and easy words • rhyme and rhythm • picture clues
For children who know the alphabet and are eager to begin reading.

Reading with Help   Preschool–Grade 1
• basic vocabulary • short sentences • simple stories
For children who recognize familiar words and sound out new words with help.

Reading on Your Own   Grades 1–3
• engaging characters • easy-to-follow plots • popular topics
For children who are ready to read on their own.

Reading Paragraphs   Grades 2–3
• challenging vocabulary • short paragraphs • exciting stories
For newly independent readers who read simple sentences with confidence.

Ready for Chapters   Grades 2–4
• chapters • longer paragraphs • full-color art
For children who want to take the plunge into chapter books but still like colorful pictures.

STEP INTO READING® is designed to give every child a successful reading experience. The grade levels are only guides; children will progress through the steps at their own speed, developing confidence in their reading. The F&P Text Level on the back cover serves as another tool to help you choose the right book for your child.

Remember, a lifetime love of reading starts with a single step!

For my wonderful husband, Mike Buckley, an amazing partner,
a supportive co-parent, and my best friend.
Thank you for taking this journey with me.
—P.M.B.

For my mom.
Thank you for always being there for me.
—A.

With grateful acknowledgment to Native American historian Julie Reed, Associate Professor of History at the Pennsylvania State University, for her help with this book.

Text copyright © 2023 by Patricia Morris Buckley
Cover art and interior illustrations copyright © 2023 by Aphelandra

Photograph credits: cover, p. 6: Buddy Mays/Alamy Stock Photo; p. 47: American Women Quarters™ Program, Wilma Mankiller Reverse © United States Mint 2021, American Women Quarters™ Program Washington Obverse courtesy of United States Mint. Used with permission.

Visit us on the Web!
StepIntoReading.com
rhcbooks.com

Educators and librarians, for a variety of teaching tools, visit us at RHTeachersLibrarians.com

Library of Congress Cataloging-in-Publication Data
Names: Buckley, Patricia Morris, author. | Aphelandra, illustrator.
Title: The first woman Cherokee Chief: Wilma Pearl Mankiller / by Patricia Morris Buckley; illustrations by Aphelandra. Portion of title: Wilma Pearl Mankiller
Description: First edition. | New York: Random House Children's Books, a division of Penguin Random House LLC, [2023] | Series: Step into reading: Step 3 book | "A biography reader"—Preliminaries. | Audience: Ages 5–8 | Summary: "The story of how Wilma Pearl Mankiller challenged gender norms introduced by settlers and became the first woman Cherokee Chief"—Provided by publisher.
Identifiers: LCCN 2022004570 (print) | LCCN 2022004571 (ebook) | ISBN 978-0-593-56850-7 (trade paperback) | ISBN 978-0-593-56851-4 (library binding) | ISBN 978-0-593-56852-1 (ebook)
Subjects: LCSH: Mankiller, Wilma, 1945–2010—Juvenile literature. | Cherokee women—Oklahoma—Biography—Juvenile literature. | Cherokee women—Oklahoma—Kings and rulers—Juvenile literature. | Cherokee Indians—Oklahoma—Politics and government—Juvenile literature. | LCGFT: Biographies.
Classification: LCC E99.C5 B8883 2023 (print) | LCC E99.C5 (ebook) | DDC 976.6004/97557—dc23

Printed in the United States of America
10 9 8 7 6 5 4 3 2   First Edition

This book has been officially leveled by using the F&P Text Level Gradient™ Leveling System.

The First Woman Cherokee Chief

Wilma Pearl Mankiller

by Patricia Morris Buckley
illustrations by Aphelandra

Random House New York

Before European settlers
came to America,
Cherokee men and women shared
the leadership of their nation.
Both men and women
made tribal rules.
Women chose the leaders
and could remove bad chiefs.
This created a balance.
Balance is very important
in Native cultures.

But white settlers
told Native people
that only men should be leaders.
The power shifted to men
for many, many years.

Then came

Wilma Pearl Mankiller,

a Cherokee woman.

She thought the chief

should be

the best person for the job,

man or woman.

Pearl (the name she went by)

was born in Oklahoma in 1945.

She lived on Cherokee lands.

Some Cherokee families

in her neighborhood

had more money than hers,

but some people struggled

to feed their families.

Her home had no indoor toilet.

No electricity.

No running water.

Like her ten siblings,
Pearl felt connected
to the land,
to nature,
and to her people.

Neighbors helped one another
by trading food and supplies.
In Cherokee,
the idea of
everyone helping one another
is called gadugi.

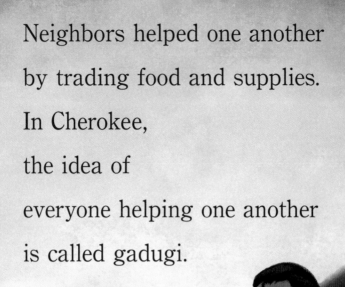

Pearl helped by doing chores.

She and her sister fetched water from a nearby spring.

They also tended the vegetable garden.

When Pearl was eleven,
a drought made life even harder.
The government started a program
that urged Native people
to move their families to cities.
Government workers put pressure
on her dad, Charley, to move.

Charley wanted to stay
on his forefathers' lands.
As a boy, he had been forced
to go to school
far from his family.
He never wanted
to leave his community again.

But he had to provide

for his family.

So they moved to San Francisco.

Pearl hated the city right away.

It was loud.

Cars screeched.

Sirens wailed.

She had to get used to

different devices,

like telephones and elevators.

She only knew country ways.

Pearl didn't like
her new school, either.
Kids laughed
at her accent and her clothes.
They made fun of her last name.

Pearl's parents had taught her
to be proud of her name.
Mankiller came from
an old title given to
Cherokee people
who protected the tribe.
Pearl tried to explain,
but kids still laughed.

Pearl's parents
let her live nearby
on her grandmother's farm
for a year.

Pearl loved

being close to nature again.

After she moved back to the city,
Pearl discovered
the American Indian Center.
There, she could be
with other Native people
from many tribes.

They played games
and held powwows.
Pearl felt more connected
to Native cultures.

In 1963,

Pearl finished high school.

By 1966, she was married

and had two daughters.

She also started college.

In 1969, Native American students
wanted to draw attention
to all the Native nations' lands
that the US government
had stolen.

A group of them
took control of Alcatraz,
an old prison on an island
near San Francisco.
It was big news!

Finally, other people
started listening
to Native Americans'
complaints.
They heard how Native people
had been stripped
of their languages,
cultures, and lands.

Pearl's brothers and sisters
joined the protest.
They lived
on the island for months.
Pearl helped raise money
for food and clothes.

The protest on Alcatraz
lasted nineteen months.
It began a new era
of Native people
standing up for their rights.

Pearl felt a fire
in her spirit.
She now knew
what she wanted to do—
help Native people
build better lives.

She helped the Pit River Tribe
fight an energy company
over stolen Native land.
She founded
the Native American Youth Center.
She helped pass a law
that meant
Native children without families
could live
with other Native families.

In 1977, Pearl moved
back to Oklahoma.
She got a job
with the Cherokee Nation.
Her daughters loved
Cherokee lands,
just as she had as a child.

One day,

while driving to Tahlequah,

the Cherokee Nation's capital,

Pearl was in a horrible car crash.

It took seventeen operations

for her to get better.

But Pearl never stopped
using the idea of gadugi
to help solve problems.
She visited Cherokee people
in Bell, Oklahoma.
Few homes had running water.
Buildings were falling apart.

Pearl listened to people
talk about how to make
their community better.
She raised money
for the projects.
Neighbors put in water pipes
and fixed up houses.
Their work was so successful
that a film was made about it.

In 1983,
the chief of the Cherokee Nation
asked her to run as his deputy.
Some people didn't want
a woman deputy chief.

They sent hate mail
and slashed her car tires.
But she won the election!

Two years later,
the chief got a new job in
Washington, D.C.
Pearl filled in as chief.

Children were important to her.

So she built day cares

and schools.

In 1987,

Pearl ran for chief.

Some Cherokees

still didn't want a woman leader.

But she reminded them

how women once

had an equal say

in running the tribe.

And people listened!
They elected Pearl
the first female chief
of the Cherokee Nation,
one of the largest tribes
in the United States.

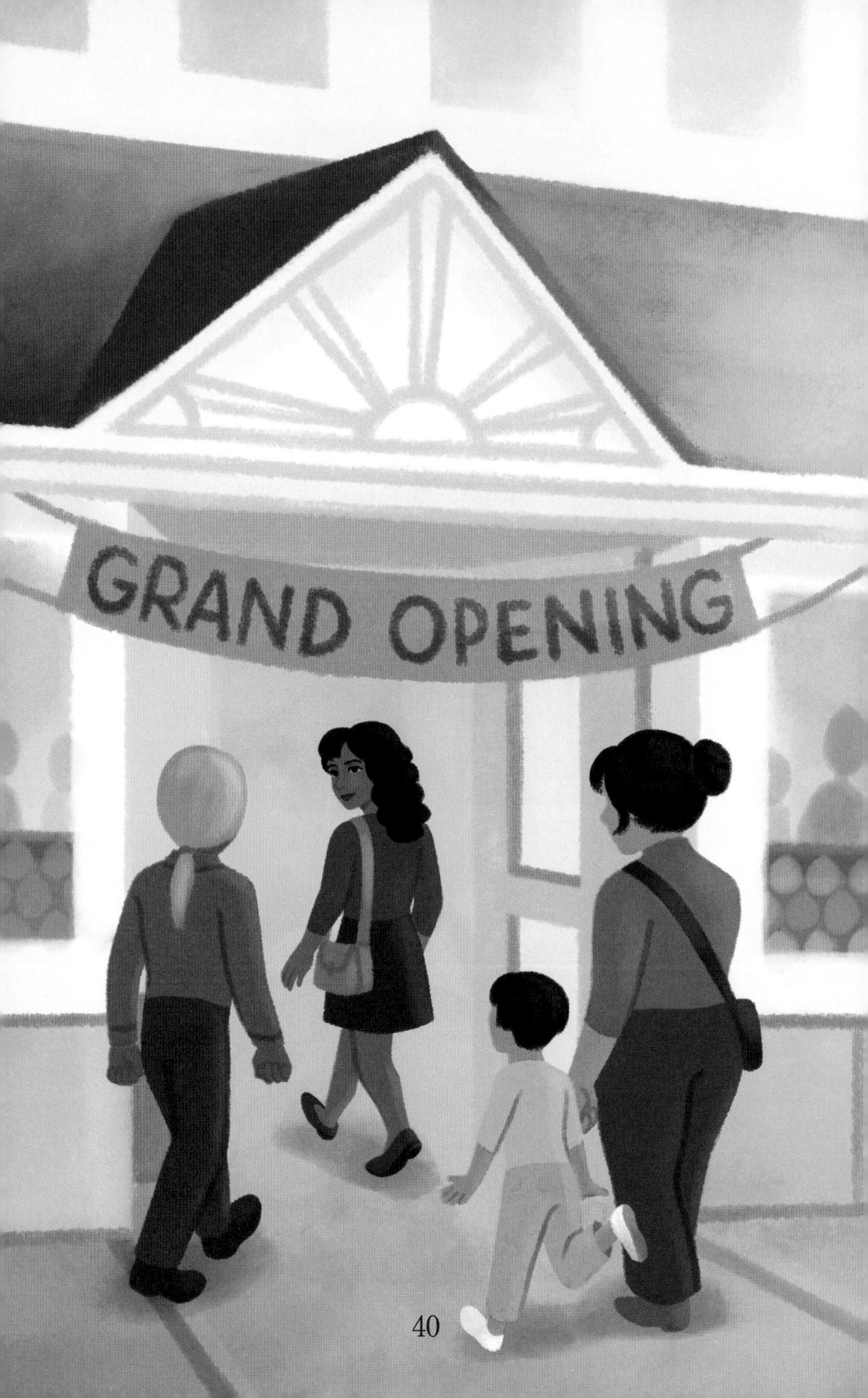
GRAND OPENING

Pearl was a good chief.

She welcomed

new businesses.

These helped make the tribe

more self-supporting.

Four years later,

she ran for another term

and won again!

Pearl encouraged her people
to make their communities better.
She oversaw projects
such as health clinics
and a job training center.
She served as chief
for ten years.

Pearl won many awards.

In 1998, President Bill Clinton

presented her with

the Presidential Medal of Freedom.

This is the highest honor

the US government can give

a nonmilitary person.

Today, there are female chiefs

in other Native nations.

Pearl was

an inspiration for them.

In celebration of her work,

she appears

on the 2022 quarter

as part of

the American Women coin series.

By the time she died in 2010,
Pearl had become a role model.
She once said,
"I have to do extra well,
because I am the first woman."
And in the many years
of helping her people,
that's exactly what
Wilma Pearl Mankiller did.